THE FOUR MARITAL PHASES

Growing & Flourishing Together as a Couple

Juwon Odutayo

JUWON ODUTAYO PUBLISHING PRESS books may be purchased in bulk for educational, business or sales promotional use. For information, please send a mail to salesandmarketing@juwonodutayo.com

ISBN: 978-978-776-959-1

PUBLISHING PRESS

Dedication

This book is dedicated to all married couples.
I salute your intentionality and commitment in making your marriage work.

Acknowledgement

No great work is ever truly accomplished alone, and this book is no exception.

To Dinma Nwobi, thank you for the push in ensuring that I prioritized this work.

To Marina Iyem Eteng, thank you for the review and the remarkable insights you added to this project.

To my gorgeous and incredible wife, words will never be enough to express my gratitude for your unwavering love and support throughout this work. From the very first thought to the final pages, you have been my most trusted sounding board, and the quiet force that kept me going till the end.

Your wisdom and thoughtful feedback have not only shaped the depth of this book but have also enriched my own understanding of the beauty and complexity of marriage.

Thank you for being my sounding board and safe place.
Thank you for doing life and love with me.
This book is as much yours as it is mine.

Table of Contents

Introduction

Marriage is a journey, not a single destination. Like the changing seasons, every marriage goes through distinct phases—some filled with excitement and discovery, others marked by challenges and uncertainty. Whether you are newlyweds navigating your first years together, a couple working through differences, or partners who have grown through the trials of time, understanding the natural progression of marriage can empower you to build a relationship that thrives.

These phases are based on the needs, dreams and personalities of the spouse. A spouse's expectations of the marriage usually activate the phases the spouse goes into per time and depending on the personality of the spouse, the phases may be short or long.

This book introduces the Four Phases of Marriage: the Learning Phase, Pushing Phase, Settling Phase, and Growing Phase.

Each phase represents a unique stage in marital development, shaped by experiences, conflicts, and the choices couples make along the way. By recognizing which phase your marriage is currently in, you gain the clarity needed to apply the right strategies, avoid common pitfalls, and strengthen your relationship intentionally.

Many couples experience frustration, disillusionment, or even stagnation in their relationship, often wondering, Is this how marriage is supposed to be? The truth is, struggles are a natural part of the marital journey, but they don't have to define your relationship. By understanding the Four Marital Phases, you will gain insight into the natural transitions of marriage, what to expect in each phase, recognize signs of growth, conflict, or stagnation in your own relationship and apply targeted strategies to nurture connection, resolve conflicts, and keep your marriage flourishing.

This book is for couples at all stages, whether you are engaged, newly married, or have been together for decades. It will equip you with practical tools to navigate the ups and downs of marriage with grace and understanding. If you're experiencing harmony, you'll learn how to sustain it. If you're struggling, you'll find hope and actionable steps to rebuild and restore your bond.

Marriage is about growth, commitment, and learning how to love and treat each other better over time. As you embark on this journey through the Four Phases, keep an open heart, embrace the process, and remember that no matter where you are, there is always a path forward.

The Time Frames of the Four Marital Phases

Each of the Four Marital Phases have estimated years attached to them, but it is important to understand that these timelines are not set in stone. While some couples may experience a phase within the typical time bracket, others may move through it more quickly or remain in it for a longer period. Marriage is a deeply personal journey, shaped by factors such as individual personalities, relationship dynamics, external circumstances, and intentional efforts to grow together.

These phases are like seasons in nature, while we expect spring to follow winter, the exact timing of when flowers bloom varies depending on climate, soil conditions, and care. Similarly, the progression of marital phases depends on how couples navigate their unique experiences.

One couple may transition from the Learning Phase to the Pushing Phase within two years, or within a month, while another may remain in the excitement and learning longer before encountering deeper challenges. Some couples may spend years in the Pushing Phase before finding strategies to reconnect, while others may recognize early warning signs and take proactive steps to move from Learning toward Growing sooner than others.

The key is not to use how long you have been married to search or determine the phase you are in, but to use the description and peculiarity of each phase to understand where you are, work through the challenges with intentionality, and nurture the connection that keeps your marriage thriving over time. From the tools and strategies shared, find out what steps you can take to grow through the phase. Please note that **the purpose of identifying these phases is not to predict exact timelines but to provide insights that help you navigate your marital journey with awareness and intention.**

No matter where you find yourself, the goal is to keep moving forward—learning, growing, and nurturing a relationship that flourishes with time.

****The estimated duration of years are only estimates. It may be less or more for each phase depending on the personalities of the partners and the peculiarities of their marriage.*

THE LEARNING PHASE

Caleb

"The match is starting in ten minutes."

"Okay." Caleb picked up the remote control and changed the TV channel.

"Is Collins coming?" Fatai asked.

"He sent me a text that he would come. You know how he is."

"If we see him, we see him. And if we don't, we don't."

Caleb's wife, Clara, walked out of the room in a red knee-length gown and a black stiletto shoe. Her face was beautifully made up and she had a cute little purse that matched her dress.

"How do I look?" She threw a quick look at her husband, spread her hands, posed, cat-walked, and waited for her husband's reaction.

"Gorgeous, as always." Caleb beamed.

"Hello Clara." Fatai smiled.

"Good afternoon, Fatai."

"Looks like you are going out."

"Yes, I have a party to attend with some friends, and I can see why your friend is choosing not to go with me."

"I am not responsible, please." Fatai lifted his two hands in the air to demonstrate his innocence."

"I will use the Rav4." Clara turned her attention back to her husband.

"Not a problem. I'm not going anywhere."

"Okay." She moved closer to him and planted a kiss on his cheeks. "All the best in your match."

"Thank you. Have fun."

"I sure will." She stepped out of the house and shut the door behind her.

"Your wife goes out a lot." Fatai remarked.

"Why do you say so?"

"Most Saturdays when I'm here, she's either not home or she is on her way out."

"Oh. I guess you're right. She is more outgoing than I am."

It's an understanding he is learning to adjust to in the marriage. Her bubbly, effervescent nature was one of the attractions for him. She knew how to dress for the occasion, and she had the skill to light up any party. It was a personality that pulled him while dating; she was a good company to have around. But now that they are married, he wasn't sure if the trait is still a pull.

"And you don't mind that she goes out a lot?"

"I don't know, I mean, it's not like she is doing anything for me in the house. If that's how she is, what can I do? I'm learning to adjust to it."

A resultant effect of Clara's outing was the lack of homemade food. It was not something he was comfortable with, but he chose to overlook because his cooking skills came in handy. He could make the kind of soups he wanted and eat his swallows. He shrugged it off.

"But if you could choose, you wouldn't mind if she stays more at home, right?"

"I don't know. I'm indifferent." He increased the volume of the TV. "The match is about to start."

"Well, maybe she will also adjust after a while."

"How so?"

"I mean, you guys are still young in this marriage, by the time the children start to come, the rules of engagement would change."

"Senior Fatai!" He giggled.

"I know what I'm talking about. My wife used to be outgoing like this when we just got married."

"Really? And now she is not?"

"Pregnancy humbled her! She slowed down and paid attention to building the family. She is at home now as we speak."

"I see."

"A woman should be homely. But I think it's just the early stages behaviour."

"Thank you, Fatai. Can we watch the match now?"

Clara

"Hello ladies." Clara joined her friends on the table and pulled out a seat. "What did I miss?"

"Hi Clara." Teju stood up and hugged her. "You haven't missed anything, we just got here too."

"Married mama!" Fidelia stretched her hands from her seat and slapped her a high five.

"My dearest sister! Na me be that o."

"You look delicious! You mean husbandman allowed you leave the house looking hot like this?"

"He is a proud husbandman. Hurry up and join the train of married folks."

"No pressure. We are coming. First task is to find a man like Caleb. That sounds like a good plan?" She laughed and turned to Daisy who was busy nursing her cocktail.

"Your husband is such a wonderful man, you know." Daisy sipped some more drink.

"I know. Honestly, I am so glad I married him."

"I was telling the girls that you may not come considering the fact that you've been out almost all the weekends this month." Daisy remarked.

"Naahhh...my husband isn't like that. He has no problem with me hanging out with my friends."

"Which is why some of us must find our own Caleb." Fidelia beckoned on one of the waiters to come and attend to Clara.

"So is he also out for a function or party?" Daisy was curious.

"He is actually at home. He is watching a soccer match with his friend. He is not the outgoing type."

"Oh okay...interesting. You are outgoing, he is not outgoing, what a beautiful combination of personalities." Teju noted.

"Madam Analyser!" Fidelia rolled her eyes at Teju. "Are there ugly personalities?"

"Just saying...you know they say, opposites attract. They somewhat complement each other."

"I totally agree." Daisy chipped in.

"That is not the case with us, though." Teju started. "My husband and I are both outgoing, in fact he is more outgoing than I am. He is at a wedding party as we speak. And from there he is going to his school alumni get-together. The fact that we are both alike in that way actually makes it fun for us."

"Meaning same or similar can also attract." Fidelia nodded.

"Well, that's my experience. And we are actually glad we are alike that way, nobody is forcing the other to be like them, I mean we are the same." Teju added.

Clara said nothing. She stared and reflected on Teju's comment. Caleb was an amazing man; he wasn't forcing her to sit at home with him and watch soccer. They both were very understanding of each other. Even though she would love that they go out together sometimes, attend events as a couple and mingle with friends, she was learning to accept Caleb for who he was and not change him to be otherwise. She believed it was the same grace her husband extended to her.

One weakness she had thought would bring a challenge in her marriage was her poor culinary skills. But Providence was magnanimous in giving her a man who could hold his own in the kitchen. She would not deny it was a major attraction for her during their courtship. Caleb made most of the meals and cooked the soups. Watching him take care of things in the kitchen and listening to him instruct her on how to mix stuff together couldn't be more romantic. He was all that he hoped and prayed for. She wouldn't ask for more.

"How does the dynamic work for you two, though? Do you sometimes wish he is outgoing or does he sometimes ask you to stay home?"

"Isn't the answer obvious? She wouldn't be here if he does?" Fidelia interjected.

Clara positioned her dish of finger foods in front of her and sipped some Chapman. "It works well for us."

"What do you mean, Fidelia?" Daisy gave her friend a puzzled look. "So, if he disapproves, you mean she does not have a mind of her own? Is that how marriage is - one partner commanding the other?"

"Don't misunderstand me. I mean, how many husbands would be this magnanimous. Clara is pretty much out of the house every weekend. The common narrative is that you get married, and you become domesticated, cut off from friends, especially *singleletic babes* like us."

"True that! We suddenly become bad influence and must not be touched with a barge pole."

"Well, I'm glad I did not marry someone with such a mindset."

THE LEARNING PHASE

Est. 1 - 7years

The Learning Phase is a phase where the partner or partners are willing to be taught and are open to receiving helpful information or instruction that can help their marriage and make them live happily together.

It is a critical stage in marriage where one or both partners exhibit a posture of openness, curiosity, and adaptability. This phase is often characterized by a willingness to seek knowledge, accept guidance, and apply practical strategies to build a stronger, healthier, and more fulfilling marital bond.

LEARNING

Description

- Newlyweds and those in the first few years of marriage are in the Learning Phase.

- They are mostly newbies and have just begun their marital journey.

- It's their first real contact with their partner's character and idiosyncrasies. Habits that the in-love state seemed to have blinded are now in full glare.

- The couple may realize they are not so alike as they probably have believed or the differences they believed were not going to cause disagreements could become major sources of conflict after all.

- So, they are willing to listen to counsel and take advice from those who have been there.

Peculiar Traits

- A fact gathering phase
- A phase of many firsts as married couples.

*first major misunderstanding as married persons,
*first pregnancy or first baby
*first Christmas together
*first family travel
*first family guest

Many firsts that reveal innate tendencies in decision-making, financial propriety, commitment, ambition, etc.

Spouses learn to

- Listen to each other.
- Bear with each other.
- Communicate effectively with each other.
- Meet each other's physical, emotional, mental, spiritual, and social needs.

Three Stages in the Learning Phase

1. The Discovery Stage

This stage could still be predominantly reflecting the in-love state. The partners are mostly thrilled about what they discover about each other. They are sometimes excited about their findings and are curious to even discover more. Some discoveries tickle them while some others rattle them.

She may be tickled that he likes his plantain diced and not sliced. And she may be rattled that he leaves the toilet seat up and not down. He may be tickled that she sings while in the shower and may be rattled she sleeps with the light on.

For the ones that rattle them, they try to adjust and accommodate. For the ones that tickle them, they make jokes about it and celebrate.

These discoveries sometimes test their level of understanding and at other times it makes them appreciate each other more. There are also discoveries in the areas of routines. They realize the need to harmonize their individual routines to make room for each other.

2. The Adjustment Stage

After a while, reality begins to set in as the in-love state begins to wane. Gary Chapman said in his book that the in-love state lasts for about two years. The pressing need to align and find a merger in habits, values, beliefs and expectations gradually begins to lead to quarrels. The needs, interests and desires (NIDs) of each spouse subtly bubble to the surface and potential conflicts may be inevitable. Again, negotiating responsibilities and work-life balance may sometimes deplete emotional connection.

Making adjustments is no child's play, ask a mother who is raising a two-year-old and has just lost her car.

3. The Identity Integration Stage

In this part of Learning Phase, spouses are curious to know how to create a shared identity as a couple while maintaining individuality. They are searching for answers, reading and possibly asking those who have had experience how they navigated.

Learners are taking notes, finding clarity and gaining skills on how to tackle challenges. They begin to apply themselves to their roles and responsibilities in the marriage. They develop a rhythm for handling challenges while strengthening their bond.

Tools & Recommended Strategies

The Learning Phase of marriage is an exciting yet foundational season where couples discover each other more deeply, adjust to new dynamics, and build a strong marital bond. It's usually a time of 'plenty' like the biblical story of Joseph when he said there would be seven years of plenty and seven years of famine. The Learning Phase can be likened to the seven years of plenty, surplus love, understanding, tolerance, excitement, forgiveness, playfulness, name them. What do you do with all that plenty? You do what Joseph did. You save. You save by creating beautiful memories, having lots of conversations, and building a strong friendship. Seven years of famine or drought followed the seven years of plenty in Joseph's story. The Egyptians navigated the drought period because they saved during the years of plenty. A Pushing Phase, synonymous to time of drought, will usually follow Learning Phase, you want to be sure you have enough (enough beautiful memories assuring each other of love and commitment) in your storehouse to manage that phase.

1. Prioritize Open and Honest Communication

Develop the habit of expressing your thoughts, emotions, and expectations clearly and respectfully. Make it okay for your partner to speak and express themselves even if their opinions differ from yours.

Take advantage of this time of 'plenty' to establish daily check-ins where you share your experiences, feelings, and needs openly without distractions. it's tougher to do that during the time of back-to-back conflict.

2. Learn and Speak Your Love Languages
This will help you express affection in meaningful ways thereby cultivating emotional and physical intimacy. Emotional intimacy fosters a deep sense of connection and trust between partners.

3. *Create Your Marital Vision*

Leverage this time of 'plenty' to create the vision you both desire for your marriage. Discuss what your goals are and where you both want to go. This would shape what you permit and what you do not permit. The time of conflict is not the ideal time to create a vision. Joesph did not save during the time of famine; he saved during the time of surplus. Create a vision during the time of 'surplus' - when you are both jolly-jolly, communication is rock-solid, emotional connection is at top level, and chemistry is strong.

4. Establish Healthy Conflict Resolution Skills

Disagreements are inevitable, but how you handle them determines the strength of your relationship.
Use the "Pause and Reflect" method—when tension arises, take a short break before responding to avoid saying hurtful things in the heat of the moment. Focus on understanding and finding solutions together.

5. Communicate Expectations & Boundaries

This is also the time to discuss your roles, responsibilities, and personal boundaries in the marriage. You do not have to copy and paste the marriage your parents, your uncles or aunties had. Create your own based on your unique tendencies and personalities. So, do what works for you.

Having conversations about finances, family involvement, household responsibilities, and personal space help set a strong foundation. Make mutual respect and understanding your goal in these conversations.

6. Invest in Growth and Learning Together

It's not impossible that you had some premarital counseling before you got married. How long was it for? Two weeks? Two months? Six months? Rarely will you find a premarital counseling that lasts up to a year. So, imagine trying to build a union you hope will last for forty, fifty or sixty years on a six-week training. It doesn't measure up. Even a first degree is for four years!

It is important to commit to personal and relational development. Read books, attending marriage workshops, and go for couples' retreat. Have a marital coach that you both respect and can listen to from time to time for valuable insights and objective perspectives. It is unwise to put a fifty-year building on a six-week training or premarital counseling.

7. Be wise about who has your ears.

What you keep beholding, you keep becoming. If your country's football team is going for the world cup, it is only wise they play friendly matches with football teams that share the same goal. If your child is preparing for the Cambridge exam, it is only wise for her to study and practice with students who share the same ambition. If your desire is to have a healthy marriage, it is only wise to find those who share the same desire or already have the same. If you know where you are going, you will understand you can't listen to just anyone. Who are you playing friendlies with? Who are your study mates? Who has your ears when it comes to marriage and family life? Who is shaping your mindsets? Where are you eating from. That they have been married for twenty-five years, or thirty-five years does not mean they know how to make it work. They might just be Settlers.

There is so much negativity out there, about men, about women, about marriage, about relationship. You have them all over social media and in all forms too. If you continue to feed on such, overtime, bitterness and cynicism would take residence in your heart, and nothing your partner does would communicate love to you.

So, if you are in the Learning Phase, be intentional about your fraternity, carefully select those you would love to have in your corner. It is a closed mindset that would select persons that only affirm or agrees with their views. Surround yourself with those who are objective and have Growth mindset. In those 'formative' years, chances are that you could be susceptible to the closest views or philosophies around you. If you consistently listen to those that are not empowering, they would start shaping your perceptions, and thoughts about marriage and your partner, which would inadvertently influence your decisions and mold your character.

Samantha Lee, licensed social worker, former wife of Tyrese, once appeared on the Hardly Initiated podcast and opened up to Ryan Catchings and Tysean Jackson about her feelings after admitting that she could have done things differently about her marriage and not divorce her husband.

"The truth about the matter is that if I had different people in my ear at that time, I would not have made that decision," Lee said.

Be wise about who has your ears because what you keep beholding, you keep becoming.

8. Seek Professional Help.

If any of the above seems difficult to execute, seek the help of a professional counselor.

A professional Family Life Coach can help you create a vision and system that is bespoke for you and your spouse. A professional counselor can help you navigate the phase you are in so you do not sabotage what you are building.

Conclusion

We are in a fast-paced generation where the patience, growth and maturity expected of people who want to do marriage are continually on a decline. Many go into marriage without adequate preparation and as a result, the required skill to live with another individual is not well-developed. It is therefore not surprising to see that, some couples' Learning Phase may not last a month before 'Pushing' or conflict begins.

Even though this material estimates Learning Phase to be within 1-7years, it is important to state that, aside personality differences, individual needs, dreams and expectations, lack of adequate preparation may affect this timeline. There are situations where married couples begin to fight in the first week and there are marriages that packed up within two weeks. This only underscores the importance of an intensive premarital program for both partners.

Secondly, the Learning Phase is not just about discovering your partner, it's about building habits, developing skills, laying a strong foundation for a lasting marriage, and becoming lifetime students of each other. Learning should never stop. Learning and Growing Phases are like Siamese twins. You grow through learning, so it's possible for your story or journey to simply be two phases: Learning Phase and Growing Phase.

THE PUSHING PHASE

Clara

"You look amazing!" Tope admired Clara. "Where did you get this dress?"

"You're the third person asking that today. My designer apparently did a good job. I will let her know."

"Just give me her number, I need to have something like this."

"Not a problem."

Clara and Tope walked to the children's section of the church to pick their children.

"I'm sending you the number right away."

"Thank you."

The two women said their final bye bye and Clara led her sons and they walked to the car park. She saw her husband from a distance in an animated conversation with his usual buddies, Fatai and Collins. She could bet they were either talking about sports or politics. Those were the two topics that excited her husband in such manner.

"Ever gorgeous Clara!" Fatai was the first to acknowledge her presence.

"Hello Fatai." She gave him a side hug and shook Collins hands. "How are you Collins?"

"Hello dear." Caleb smiled at his wife.

I'm good." Collins replied. "We were just talking about how powerful today's sermon was."

"*Abeg*! Tell that to someone who doesn't know you guys!" She opened the car door for her sons to go in.

Her response evoked laughter from the two men.

"So, I will see you guys later." Caleb shook their hands and dismissed them.

"We are right behind you." Fatai gave him a thumbs up and crossed the road to where Collins parked his car.

The drive home was quiet, as usual. Conversations between her and her husband were scarce lately. When they were done with the appearances they gave in public, they reverted to their silence mode. That morning, again, Caleb got out of bed late, and it irked her.

No matter how many times she complained, he never listened. She gave him a piece of her mind again and the silence that enveloped the car became the consequence.

“Let me even see you make the effort! You have absolutely nothing to do in the morning aside, get up from bed, brush your teeth and take a bath! I prepare the boys, I make the breakfast, clean the house and we still get ready before you. It doesn’t make sense.”

Caleb cast a quick look at the back seat and saw the boys were fast asleep. “Last time I checked, you are not the pastor who says the opening prayers, so I don’t understand what the fuss is about.”

“Eleven years and the same complaint! Come on! All I ask for is sleep early and wake up early so we are not late to church, how difficult can that be?”

“Lateness is what you are giving me hell about, but has it crossed your mind that there are men who don’t go to church at all and their wives are not making their lives hell? What should those women do? Commit suicide?”

“I was aware enough not to marry one of them.”

“Congratulations! Maybe if you also make some effort and meet the needs of your husband, who knows, lateness may no longer be an issue.”

“Are we talking about sex again? You never cease to amaze me!”

"Be thankful that you and your family drive to church together because there are those who do not have that privilege. Ten minutes lateness, for goodness' sake!"

"Twenty minutes! Point of correction."

That was how they left for church that morning. Actually, it was how they left for church most Sunday mornings. Other days had their peculiar quarrels, but Sundays' challenge was usually about Caleb's lateness. It always rubbed Clara off the
wrong way. She volunteered in the protocol's department, and it was important she got to church early. It seemed that was not an assignment Caleb prioritized.

Clara looked at the rear-view mirror as they entered their compound and saw Collins' car right behind them. She threw a puzzled look at her husband as he turned off the car engine, "You didn't tell me Fatai and Collins were coming home with us."

"Oh, I forgot. Man City has a match this afternoon. They are watching the match at our place."

Clara was livid. "But you could have told me!"

"It was right there at the car park in church that the decision was made. What chance did I have to mention it when you were busy on your phone all through the drive home?"

Clara fumed as she got out of the car. "It's just not fair!"

Caleb had the annoying habit of bringing guests over without notifying her. Maybe she didn't complain at first because she thought it was something he would outgrow when they fully understood each other but it was apparent a leopard could not change its spots. Each time she complained, he would apologize but would do it again.

She was not repulsive to receiving his friends, she just asked to be notified so she could prepare. He expected her to entertain the guests but didn't care if they had enough at home for such entertainment and if she was up to it.

Again, she had been complaining about doing all the house chores alone, with no assistance or support from him. She prepared their meals, washed the clothes, cleaned the house, nursed their nine- and five-year old, did the school runs and attended parent-teacher meetings by herself. All these she did in addition to her nine to five. The tasks were getting her stressed out and were beginning to take a toll on her health, but her husband couldn't be bothered. Some help in form of a maid or a having a cousin live with them would go a long way if he was not ready to team up with her but Caleb reckoned her concerns to the cold.

Caleb

"The post was hilarious! You didn't see it?" Fatai threw Caleb a puzzled look

"When do I have the time to go on IG?" Caleb hissed.

"You should go there sometimes." Collins chipped in. "It was the picture we took when we were in 200 level."

"With Belinda and Rasheedat?"

"Yes!" Fatai cackled again.

"How dare you?" It was Caleb's turn to laugh as he pretended to punch his friend. "I hope my wife is not following you on IG."

"She is not. You have nothing to worry about." Collins reassured.

"Did it bring back memories you think you had forgotten?" Fatai teased.

"Belinda showed my brother Shege Promax." Collins laughed some more.

"Nahhh... it wasn't meant to be. Where is the babe now?"

"That is the gist. Two hours after I posted, she was in the Comment section asking after you."

"You don't mean it!"

"You want me to show you her comment?"

"Abeg! I don't have the time. My wife is here." He pointed in his wife's direction.

"By the way, we are coming to watch Man City match at your place." Fatai announced.

"Why? Don't you have a house? Please go and watch in your house or go to Collins' house."

"Are you stopping us from coming to your house now? Or is your wife disapproving of us."

"Of course not!" He lied.

He always loved the company of his friends, but his wife always complained they ate too much and made a lot of noise.

"So, what is the problem?"

Before Caleb could wing a reply, Clara joined them.

"Ever gorgeous Clara!" Fatai was the first to acknowledge her presence.

"Hello Fatai." She gave him a side hug and shook Collins hands. "How are you Collins?"

"Hello dear." Caleb smiled at his wife.

"I'm good." Collins replied. "We were just talking about how powerful today's sermon was."

"*Abeg*! Tell that to someone who doesn't know you guys!" She opened the car door for her sons to go in.

Her response evoked laughter from the two men.

"So, I will see you guys later." Caleb shook their hands and dismissed them.

"We are right behind you." Fatai gave him a thumbs up and crossed the road to where Collins parked his car.

Caleb started the car and the gloom that enveloped the car when they left the house in the morning returned.

What was the point of coming to church angry every Sunday? He thought. *Once I figure out the excuse to give the children, I would stop this hypocritical charade.*

The last time they were sexually intimate was six weeks ago. If he lamented, she made it seem all he thought about was sex. He would wake up with morning wood on Sundays, but by the time he stretched on the bed to cuddle his wife, she had left to the spare room to pray. He would turn and turn on the bed struggling to control himself before getting up. He tried masturbating a few times but was not happy with the feeling it left him. So, he stayed longer in bed till he was sure he would not embarrass himself when he got up or when he was out in public.

If she was not out early to pray, she was not in the mood. If headache was not the excuse, body pains would be it. At nights she was tired, in the mornings she had to pray. The excuses were never ending. *Here I am with a beautiful and desirable wife, but I can't touch her. I am continually starved of sex.*

THE PUSHING PHASE

Est. 8 - 17years

The Pushing Phase is a phase where the spouse or spouses exert measured pressure to get their partner to treat each other better, strengthen their commitment, invest more in the relationship and commit to the marriage and are unrelenting about it.

Pushers are spouses who after a long period of bearing and long-suffering realize that the marriage is for the long haul and therefore become very expressive about their needs and the needs of the marriage.

Description

- The Pushing Phase is a phase where the partner or partners become open about their expectations of their spouses and of the marriage.

- The Pushing Phase is not usually about control; rather, it is about lovingly but firmly advocating for what is best for the marriage.

- It's a phase characterized by back-and-forth disagreements on several issues ranging from finance to parenting to life goals and sex.

- The spouse who initiates the push is often driven by a strong belief that their partner is capable of more, more effort, more emotional presence, more responsibility, or more engagement.

- Pushers are unwilling to keep quiet about their needs or the marriage needs. It's a push or call for deeper investment in the marriage, urging their partner to spend more quality time together, take responsibility for unresolved issues, prioritize the relationship over external distractions, or participate in counseling, mentorship, or marriage-building activities.

Peculiar Traits

The partner or partners usually have

- not only had a taste of their partner's personality but a whole meal of it.
- been hurt by several tendencies from their spouse
- had a fair share of unresolved fights and conflicts.
- experienced a drought of the good times they used to have.
- *'seen-finish'* their spouse. The syndrome has taken residence in the marriage, and they are uncomfortable with it.
- had unpleasant confrontations. Spouses in this phase do not cease to express their minds and tell their spouses what the ideal marriage should look like and how theirs is a far cry from the ideal.
- experienced discomfort and some level of resistance when they expressed their needs and concerns.

Three Stages in the Pushing Phase

1. The Wake-Up Stage

In this stage, partners begin to become more expressive in confronting patterns of dissatisfaction or their unmet needs in the marriage.

They recognize that certain behaviors or dynamics are hindering their connection and happiness. One or both partners decide that change is necessary and start exerting measured pressure for growth and improvement.

This stage is characterized by:

- Heightened awareness of marital gaps
- Desire to communicate unmet expectations
- Tensions due to unaddressed concerns or issues being swept under the carpet.

2. *The Adjustment & Negotiation Stage*

This stage involves negotiating the changes necessary for a healthier and more fulfilling relationship. Both spouses may face pushback or resistance as they try to establish new patterns of communication, responsibilities, and emotional connection. The key challenge here is maintaining persistence without creating hostility.

This stage is characterized by:

- Increased but measured tension during change efforts
- Emotional highs and lows as partners renegotiate roles
- Struggles with accountability and follow-through.

- *The Renewal or Redirection Stage*

This stage represents a turning point where the couple either successfully renews their commitment with stronger relational dynamics or faces the possibility of separation due to unresolved conflicts. Spouses who successfully navigate this stage often experience deeper intimacy and greater teamwork. Spouses who are unable to successfully navigate this stage may begin to weigh their options whether to **settle** or leave.

This stage is characterized by:

- Strengthened emotional resilience in the marriage
- Clearer or murky communication patterns
- Increased mutual respect or contempt in the marriage.

Types of Pushing

There are two major types of Pushing. They are:

1. Pushing to have your way
2. Pushing to have a blissful marriage

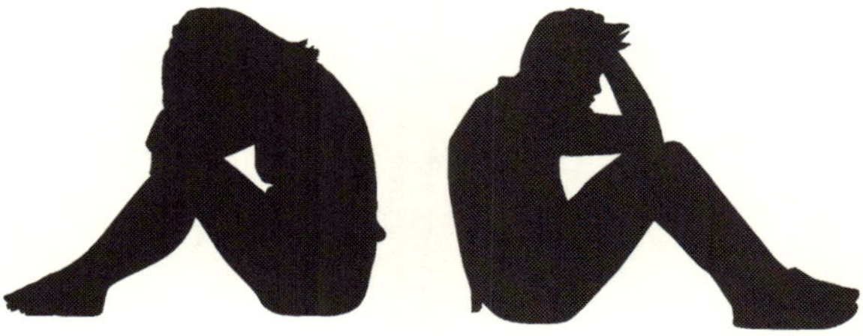

What are they Pushing for and against?

They push against:	They push for:
neglect *	* attention
monotony *	* more intimacy
accepting the status quo *	* more kindness
settling for less *	* more date nights
purposeless marriage *	* more romance
unfair treatment *	* a better marriage

Pushers may take advantage of opportunities that help point their partners to their needs.
Such opportunities may include:

- Couples' meetings
- Marriage seminars or webinars
- Couples' retreat
- Relationship messages or videos
- TV programs

They may also drop subtle messages about their concerns, in hope that their partners would pick them and respond positively.

Styles of Pushing

1. Silent Treatment
2. Nagging and complaining
3. Confrontations
4. Setting Ultimatums
5. Words of Affirmation
6. Setting boundaries and consequences
7. Reporting to a third party
8. Unavailability
9. Prayers or spiritual interventions
10. Conversations

The Pushing Phase could be a time of...

1. Mental Ease	1. Mental Stress
2. Emotional Stability	2. Emotional Disconnection

Pushing is usually inevitable and unavoidable.
While uncomfortable, the Pushing Phase can be a catalyst for breakthroughs in a marriage. Without it, many relationships would remain in an unfulfilling cycle of passivity, resentment, or unmet expectations.

When a couple is able to push with a growth mindset, open to new perspectives, willing to consider their partner's needs and concerns, it leads to mental ease and emotional stability. Such couples move from the Pushing Phase to Growing Phase. They simply grow from there and continue to learn and discover each other in the marital journey. They experience greater emotional connection, a renewed sense of commitment, healthier boundaries and clearer expectations. They both enjoy personal and relational transformation.

However, when a couple is unable to listen and consider each other, Pushing can bring mental stress and emotional disconnection. The conflict could be unending in such situations, and it may threaten the sustainability of the marriage.

The Overlap Between Learning & Pushing

Marriage is not a rigid, step-by-step journey where one phase ends before another begins. Instead, the Four Marital Phases—Learning Phase, Pushing Phase, Settling Phase, and Growing Phase—often overlap, creating a complex and dynamic experience for couples. This overlap occurs because relationships are influenced by personal growth, external pressures, and how each partner navigates challenges and transitions.

While the Learning Phase is usually characterized by excitement, discovery, and adaptation as couples adjust to married life, friction often arises, pushing couples into the Pushing Phase, where differences become more apparent, and conflicts emerge. Some couples may still be learning how to communicate and understand each other while simultaneously experiencing moments of tension and resistance.

This overlap implies, one moment, a couple enjoys deep connection, and the next, they are clashing over expectations. If they recognize that conflict is a natural part of growth, they can navigate this period with patience and a willingness to resolve issues constructively rather than seeing disagreements as signs of incompatibility.

Tools & Recommended Strategies

As mentioned above, Pushing has the potentials to bring mental ease and emotional stability. It is an inevitable and integral part of any love relationship. It is what several people may call conflict. But it is mostly a deep desire from either partner to feel seen, and their needs acknowledged and validated.

Every individual has Needs, Interests and Desires (NIDs) which are mostly drawn from their values and goals in life. When individuals come into marriage, they do not reckon marriage as a death to their NIDs, rather they see their partners as enhancers and their unions a platform whereby their NIDs would be fulfilled, their goals get a better prospect of being achieved and their values improved. Any perceived threat to these Needs, Interests, Desires or concerns makes the partners edgy, uncomfortable, and defensive.

When the needs, interests and desires of two people differ and clash in a way that it impacts their relationship and unsettles their comfort, tensions will arise. Marital conflict or Pushing happens when series of concerns and interests have not been given the desired attention.

As long as two people, from two different backgrounds, upbringing and varied significant emotional experiences, in a love relationship or marriage have conversations, express their views, share their concerns and NIDs, there will be situations for disagreement and conflict. It is mostly unavoidable.

With a growth mindset, they can open themselves up to new learning and perspectives and as a result Push wisely. But with a fixed mindset, they may hurt each other and jeopardize the love they share. The challenge lies in **HOW** they Push. Depending on how the partners Push, the marriage can move towards growth, or it can nosedive.

Pushing gives both parties the opportunities to:

- express their views and perspectives on issues
- listen to each other and
- understand each other better

In a Pushing phase, the following strategies are recommended:

1. Choose conversations.

Being expressive is good but there is a difference between confrontations and conversations.

Conversation is an exchange of ideas, an open-ended dialogue to understand perspectives, and connect with the other person. It is usually calm and respectful. Its goal is to seek collaboration and get clarity.

Confrontation, on the other hand is direct, intense and emotionally charged. It is usually fueled by anger and has a semblance of judicial proceeding. It creates tension and makes the other person defensive.

Confrontation says, 'You spent all the money and didn't even think of other needs!'

That's definitive, conclusive and accusatory. The only reaction possible is to be defensive and prove the jury wrong.

Conversation would take the same issue and say, 'May I know why you made so and so expense?'
That's enquiry-like, curious, and expressing a desire to gain understanding. It presents the issue as something to be resolved.

Five Quick Steps for Effective Conversations

i. Find a calm and relaxed time, and place.

Trying to have a conversation in the heat of an argument is not likely going to work.

ii. *Set the tone for safety and partnership*

Say these words to each other before you start:

- "We are on the same team, and our goal is understanding, not winning."
- "Your feelings and needs matter to me, and I am here to listen with an open heart."

- "We will work through this together, with kindness, patience, and honesty."

Then take turns to speak and listen.

The diagram in the next page explains how the Speaker should speak and the posture or attitude of the Listener.

For the Speaker: You NFN

Start your conversation with the phrases in each balloon; "I noticed..." "I feel...." or "I need..." **You NFN**

For the Listener: You AVA

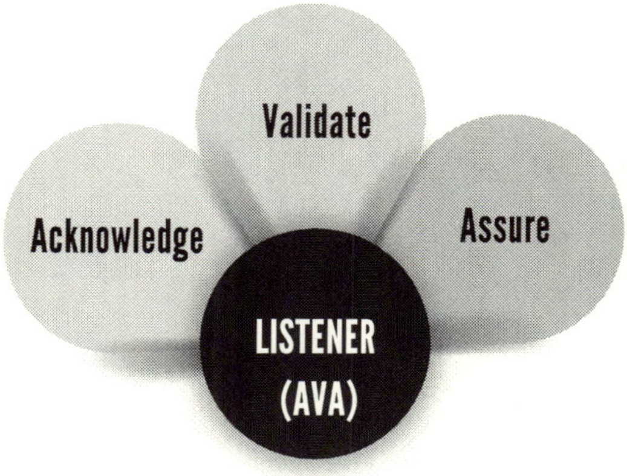

While your partner speaks, avoid complaining, defending of judging. Simply do what you see in the three balloons: You Acknowledge, Validate and Assure. **You AVA**

The Speaker NFN. The Listener AVA

iii. Explore solutions together with the question:
"How can we meet this need in a way that works for both of us?"
"How can we resolve this issue in a way that satisfies both of us?"
"Tell me two ways I can treat you better going forward."

iv. *Express Gratitude*
"Thank you for listening and showing understanding. It means a lot to me."

v. *Make it a habit.*
Make it a biweekly or monthly routine.

Three simple ways to know whether you are having conversations or confrontations are:
i. Your Intent: Clarity or Condemnation?
ii. Your Tone & Approach: Respectful or Judgmental?
iii. Your Outcome & Impact: Resolution/Understanding or Conflict?

2. Be Willing to Compromise

It is true that unmet expectations often lead to frustration and emotional withdrawal. Clearly communicate your needs and desires but be willing to compromise to embrace a resolution that satisfies both of you.

Use the "Win-Win Method" – You both write down your top two needs, then find a middle ground that respects both perspectives.

3. Seek Professional Help

If you realize you are not making a headway or if there is no bandwidth from either person to sit and talk, then get help. Do not struggle alone, help is available. Seek help from a marriage coach, therapist, or trusted mentor who can uncover underlying issues and equip both of you with practical tools.

Conclusion

Since growth often comes with discomfort, the Pushing Phase is typically met with some level of resistance. A spouse may feel pressured, defensive, or reluctant to change. However, when done correctly, this phase fosters transformation rather than conflict. The Pushing Phase is not a sign of failure, it's a phase leads to deeper love and understanding when handled well.

The Pushing Phase does not have to be the breaking point of your marriage. With intentional effort, patience, and the right strategies, you can turn conflicts into opportunities for deeper understanding and lasting connection. Instead of fighting against each other, choose to fight for your marriage and you'll emerge stronger, wiser, and more united than ever.

THE SETTLING PHASE

Clara

"He is taking my silence and the fact that I no longer complain to mean everything is fine. Seems like he likes how things are and can't be bothered that I am unhappy."

When Clara came for counseling, her first intention was how to get her husband to join her so they could both get help. After her first counseling session, she spoke to him and expressed her dissatisfaction, but it all fell on deaf ears. He believed her intention was to force his hand to do her bidding and he didn't want to feel controlled by her anymore.

'Where does that leave you?"

"I feel helpless. I feel he pushed me to the point where I have no energy left to complain. So when he strolls in at odd hours, he is pleased that I am not furious like I used to be. He is happy he can go about his 'businesses' without anyone breathing down his neck."

"It seems he is okay with the status quo then."

"But I am not. I am unhappy."

"Do you think he is happy?"

"I wish he is not. I really wish he is not. That way we will both be on the same page seeking help. But he looks happy. I see him just carrying on without me. He must be happy."

"And you don't want him to?"

"That's not what I mean."

"What do you mean?"

"He said, I am his happy place, how is he now happy without me? I want to be happy too."

"What will make you happy?"

"When my husband pays attention to me. I have needs, needs for companionship and connection. It's frustrating being in the same house with your significant other and you don't talk. This is not what I imagined my marriage would be."

"I see."

"I'm praying he comes around and show that he wants things back the way they used to."

"And if he doesn't?"

"He has to. Maybe he is going through a phase. I believe he will tire out and come around."

"And if he doesn't?"

"If he doesn't? Honestly, I don't know. I don't know how I can continue like this. I'm depressed most of the times. I don't know if I can continue like this."

"Continue like?"

"The dreariness in the home is suffocating."

"Are there ways you can pay attention to you if he is choosing not to? I mean, are there ways you can create your own happiness, and meet your own needs by yourself?"

"Doesn't that mean I would have to leave him? Wouldn't that be asking if I can be single again?"

"Are you saying that being married means giving another the responsibility to make you happy?"

"If you love someone, wouldn't your preoccupation be that they are happy?"

"What if they don't have the capacity to? And if your frustration stems from him not paying attention to you or meeting your needs, what are your options?"

"I don't know. How can I be living like a single person while in a marriage?"

"It depends on what you want. You can be in the marriage and create your own happiness. You can also leave the marriage and create your own happiness. You have a choice. What do you want?"

"To be happy. To live a fulfilled life of purpose. I want to flourish and live a life of impact."

What's stopping you? Are you underestimating the power you have?"

"I guess I can find ways of creating my own happiness in the marriage and stop expecting him to make me happy."

"Tha's an option."

"You know, if I hadn't come for your meeting, I wouldn't have been able to name my situation. Now I don't know if I feel worse or better by coming."

"Why?"

"I had thought our state was normal, that my unhappiness was not uncommon."

"How so?"

"We already resigned to the state of things. We have been like that for a couple of years. My husband is not a bad man; he is hardworking, pays the bills, and provides for the home."

"And?"

It's But, not and."

"But..."

"I know we are not fine."

"We don't talk. Our emotional connection is dead. We don't know what's going on in each other's lives."

"You said everything was fine."

"I assumed after about twenty-eight years of marriage, it's okay for monotony to set in and for spouses to be like that."

"Like what?"

"Like just be there, like housemates... the dreariness, the lack of emotional connection, the dullness, just going through the motions, living together, but living separate lives, not involved in each other's lives."

"I see."

"You know, on the outside, we really look okay. I mean, you can't see us at an event and suspect that we are not okay. Okay, maybe you can because you are a therapist, but an average man can't tell that it's been over twenty-six months we were sexually intimate or that we do not talk once we are inside the house."

"You don't have anyone living with you?"

"I told you all the children are out."

"I mean, no relation, or maid?"

"My cousin comes around once in a while. Our first-born visits during the holidays. That's about it."

"So, you assumed this state was normal?"

"I guess we have found a way to function and do our duties regardless of how far apart we feel."

"I see."

"That's the phase you described as Settling. I have settled. I can confidently say that we settled - publicly endearing, privately unloving, in your words."

"But it's working for both of you, is it not?"

It's not. I know there is a void. I know it's possible to have better, but I don't know how. I know I am only waiting for our last born to get a job outside of town and then make a move. I have been nursing the thoughts of leaving. I want to be happy."

"What if happiness is not the purpose of marriage?"

"Is the purpose gloom and depression? Was the institution created to make one lose the zest to life? Like all the dreams and aspirations I had as a single lady, were they supposed to die because I got married?"

"No one said so. But why did you stop chasing those dreams when you got married? Why did you abandon the things that made for your happiness when you got married?"

"I guess...I thought...I don't know...I didn't realize. Maybe I was expecting him to make them happen for me."

"I see."

"It was the promise he made to me."

"Okay."

"If there are couples enjoying their marriage after thirty or forty years, why is mine different?"

"Sometimes our state or position is an outcome of the choices we made."

Silence.

"So, what do you want to do?"

"The interesting part of this is that we are marriage counselors in our local church. Isn't that laughable?"

"You mentioned your state isn't that obvious to the public. It explains why. Maybe you have perfected your public outlook and learnt to cope so well that your ache for a change is not so apparent."

"We are so settled in the rot."

"The Settling Phase is somewhat deceptive. It's a façade. You look okay but you both know something died. You no longer care. You no longer bother."

"Very true. I have no expectations of Caleb any longer, it's a coping mechanism I deployed to avoid the constant disappointments. And when I don't get disappointed, the fights reduce. I thought that was growth or maturity. I can tell it's same for him, nothing I do or don't do moves him."

"Where does that leave you?"

"He used to care. He used to be concerned about my well-being but it's different now. It seems we have our best times when we are away from each other. We don't miss each other when either of us travel. And whenever we are together, we are always looking for the events or travels to make us leave again."

"Hmmn."

"I don't look forward to going home, I know he doesn't either. Visiting the children always excites us because it's an opportunity to be away from each other. Once we are back home, we can't wait for the opportunity to leave again."

"Wow."

She caught a tear drop.

"But I can't live like this for the rest of my life."

“We can look at the options available together.”

“I don’t think there are many options. I have the power to create my own happiness, you said. I simply have to decide whether I want to do that while inside the marriage or outside the marriage.”

“Okay.”

Caleb

"Should I put this in the box?"

"What's that?"

"Your blue TM."

"Yes, put it in the box." David folded the shirt and dropped it in the traveling box.

"For how long will you be away for this time?"

"One week, son. Any problems?"

"No. Just wanted to know."

"Why? It's not like you live here, so what will my absence do to you?"

"But your wife is here. I wonder how she fairs without you around."

"You think she misses me? Did she complain about my traveling?" Caleb zipped the box and placed it by the wardrobe. "Your mum is fine. I think she would be fine."

"Are you sure?" David placed his dad's laptop bad on the box and crossed to sit on the bed.

"I'm sure." Caleb stood up. "I think we are done. Thanks for helping with this." He took a step towards the door. "Are you coming?" He noticed his son did not get up.

"Can I ask you a question?" David locked eyes with his father.

"What is it?" He stood by the door and waited.

"Can I ask you a question?"

"Of course! What is it?" He was getting impatient.

"Please, can you sit down?"

"How will my sitting affect my answer?" He walked back and joined his son on the bed. "What is it?"

"Is there another woman?"

Caleb laughed and stared at the brown carpet. He placed his phone by his side on the bed and gently raised his head to look at his son. "Why did you ask?"

David did not flinch. "Just answer my question, dad. Is there another woman?"

"Maybe if I know why you are asking, I will be able to answer you properly."

"It's not a difficult question, dad. It only requires a simple Yes or No."

"Okay. No, there's no other woman."

"And that's the truth?"

"Yes. That's the truth." He sighed. " What's the problem?"

"It's you and mum."

"What did she tell you?"

"Nothing. Is there something she should tell me or that I should know?"

"I don't know. I don't poke my nose in your conversations."

"She doesn't have to tell me anything, dad. I see both of you. You don't talk!"

"That's coming from someone who doesn't live here. How did you know we don't talk?"

"I've been home for three days now, you two have not exchanged more than three sentences."

"Really? You must be a monitoring spirit to know."

David ignored his comment and continued. "You are not in the same space per time; if she is in the bedroom, you are in the living room. If she is in, you are out. Then this your traveling...." He took a deep breath. "It bothers me."

"What about it? Why does it bother you? How do you mean?"

"For the about two years now, if not more, your trips have been one too many, especially to Abuja."

Caleb chuckled and sat more comfortably on the bed. "They are work trips, David."

"I want to believe that but it's difficult when I see how you and mum relate with each other."

Caleb sighed. He stretched and pulled one of the pillows for support.

His son was right. In as much as he tried to deny the situation he was in with his wife, there were too many signs to prove him wrong. They were able to maintain status quo for two years now because all their sons had left home. It made it easy to adjust and settle in the rot. But David's frequent visit home had exposed them, and his wedding plans had ripped open what he thought was well covered.

David read his father's countenance. "What happened Dad?" He probed gently. "What happened to the two of you?"

Caleb tried to fix his face. "Nothing happened. We are fine." He looked away afraid his son could see the lie.

It wasn't that anything happened. He reflected. And when he thought about it, he wished there was something that happened so they could have some culprit, some demon to nail their despondent marriage on. But there was none. Adultery didn't lead them to this state. Domestic violence wasn't responsible for the gloom. There was no abuse. There was no definitive conflict. All he could remember was after a while they began to care less about each other.

"We can talk about it, Dad. I will understand." David tried to encourage his dad.

Caleb simulated a smile. *I don't think you will understand, David. It's not an incident; it's a potpourri of several things. You won't understand.* He rubbed his temple as the emotions overwhelmed him. *Your mum and I couldn't find a middle ground with our desires. She was always out and didn't care about how lonely and abandoned I felt. I wanted her to choose me, but she preferred her friends. When I complained she played the victim, nagged and cried that I knew she was outgoing before I married her. You won't understand, David.*

I never imagined marriage would be the place where I would have to beg and beg to be intimate with my wife. I didn't even have that experience as a single man. I came into marriage and sex became a reward for good behaviour. And the judge and jury for my good behaviour was your mum - I lost the case before hearing. Whenever I was lucky, it felt like she was doing me a favour. I got sick of it.

I got sick of it and stopped begging. When I stopped, we went for seven straight months without sex and your mum wasn't bothered. It scared me.

I began to adjust. I noticed when I expressed a need, we fought and when I didn't, we had peace. I wanted peace, so I stopped expressing my needs.

I was so grateful my mum trained her boys well; God bless her soul. I could coax the best from every ingredient. I could take the humblest of ingredients and turn them into a feast. I was not that husband who had the luxury of asking his wife to make him a special meal. Whatever I desired, I walked into the kitchen and made it. It used to be a joy at the beginning. The kitchen was one of the places we created the most amazing memories. She would sing melodious tunes while my hands moved with the confidence of a painter, each stroke measured, each color intentional.

But when it became a task, a necessity, the passion died, and I started cooking for survival. And when I didn't cook, I went out to eat. The abandonment was too unbearable, I sought solace in discovering many food joints. I started trying various cuisines, it made me go out a lot, it became fun discovering restaurants. I began to look for work travels, too. I felt, since I wasn't really wanted at home, what was the point staying?

I would not deny there had been a couple of flings as a result but it was only my way of adjusting to the state of the marriage. Sleeping in hotel rooms came with their peculiar attachments. I have indulged a few times. There are no guarantees that will stop soon if we continue like this.

My friends are having a party in Abuja this weekend, I would choose this trip a hundred times over this hellhole we call marriage. I mean, it's not like she cares about where I go or who I see. It's convenient for both of us. I make sure I do not question her too about her whereabout. it's a good strategy for both of to be free to do whatever we want and it's working perfectly well. The marital status is essential for social standing, but the communication gap is important for individual freedom. We have a good arrangement. We are fine, son.

"There's nothing to understand, David." His smile was genuine this time.

"Dad..." David hesitated.

"Son..." Caleb distracted himself by pilfering with his phone.

"I sense you are unsure about sharing your concerns with me."

"I don't want you worrying over us. We are fine. Your mum and I are in a good place. We are not fighting, we talk. And as you can see, there's peace around here."

David ignored the pretense. "If you can't trust me enough to share with, would you like to speak to a counselor? I can speak with the one preparing Nelly and I for marriage."

"You both have started counseling?"

"Yes. Mum referred someone to us."

"That's nice."

"Would you like me to give you his number?"

"David, why are you doubting what I'm telling you? You know, you are in other words saying I'm lying? We are okay. We don't need to speak to any counselor."

"One more question, Dad."

"What is it again?" His patience was wearing thin.

"If I pray to have the kind of relationship you both have now when I am your age, would you say Amen?"

Caleb raised his head and looked at his son.

"Answer me truthfully, Dad. Would you say Amen?"

"No." Caleb stood up.

"Thank you. I will text you the counselor's number." He stood up.

"Okay." He stepped towards the door. "Let's go and get something to eat."

THE SETTLING PHASE

Est. 18+years

The Settling Phase is a phase where one or both partners, having seen no positive change, become tired of Pushing, and have resolved to settle for what has been meted out to them.

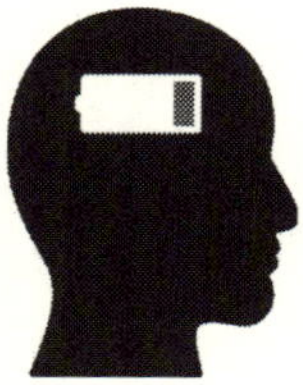

It is a critical point in the marriage where one or both partners, having exerted significant effort to improve their relationship in the Pushing Phase, begin to feel emotionally exhausted and resigned.

In this phase, the hope for meaningful change diminishes, and couples gradually stop fighting for growth and deeper connection in their marriage. Instead, they settle into a rhythm that feels emotionally distant, unfulfilling, or stagnant, simply accepting things as they are.

Description

They have seen that their partners are set in their ways and all efforts to make them

- consider another perspective,
- grow to become better,
- drop unhealthy patterns or
- be more present and intentional

yielded no result.

They weighed the options, and they resolved they would rather shrug it off and settle than walk out of the marriage.

- Settlers are those spouses who could no longer be bothered about their needs being met or not.
- While couples in the Pushing Phase may nag and scream obscenities at each other, couples in the Settling Phase believe, *'I've seen that, done that*!' They consider themselves 'stronger and more mature', so they no longer express any emotion or feeling.

They believe expressing emotions or needs is a sign of weakness and it communicates that they still care. Since they no longer care or can't be bothered, they shrug off whatever their partners do and ignore.

- Conversations become routine and transactional, lacking depth and intimacy.

- Their expectations of their partners have dropped; they usually could be locked in neutral when their needs are met and are indifferent when their needs are not met.

- Overtime, they become cynical about love and marriage.

- They could sneer at young loves (Learners) and jeer at their 'exaggerated' romantic gestures.

- They are mostly the ones who are quick to warn Learners to enjoy their honeymoon while it lasts and that the bliss they dream of is a façade.

- Efforts to address conflicts decline. Partners may stop expecting change and instead learn to tolerate what once bothered them.

Peculiar Traits

- Many times, they have the appearance of a perfect, happy marriage but it is a position they have taken and perfected for 'peace's sake'.

- Over time, unspoken frustrations build up, leading to internalized resentment. While outward conflict may decrease, unresolved hurts linger beneath the surface.

- To cope with dissatisfaction, partners may focus on work, children, friendships, or hobbies, subtly shifting their attention away from the marriage.

- They pride themselves in how long they have been married and find it difficult to take advice from anyone.

- In several churches, it is not uncommon to find Settlers as marriage counselors or in the family unit where they teach intending couples and newly married couples.

- Many times, they profile you before they can listen to you; how long has he been married, what does he have, what does he do?

Settling is a common feature in many African homes than in the West. It is commonplace to find several in the West move on to another relationship once they feel unhappy or emotionally disconnected. But most Africans revere the marriage institution and as a result, would work tirelessly to keep it.

This explains why many would choose Settling instead of walking out. Culture and other social factors contribute to this mindset.

Settlers somewhat have faith/hope that their partners will see the light someday and time will turn around for them. For many African women, they find solace in religion and embark on unending prayers hoping for divine intervention in their marriage.

For others who are unable to pull strength from religion, they may engage in unhealthy habits to distract themselves from the gloom in their marriage. Some men may resort to drinking as a coping mechanism.

Three Stages in the Settling Phase

1. The Resignation Stage

At this stage, spouses experience emotional fatigue from years of pushing for changes that have not materialized. They have nothing left in the tank to push or fight. They often resign themselves to accepting their partner's behavior and the current state of their marriage as unchangeable.

This stage is characterized by:

- Emotional withdrawal and reduced expectations
- Fewer attempts to initiate difficult conversations
- Increased focus on individual activities rather than shared ones.

2. The Co-Existence Stage

Spouses in this stage may develop a functional but emotionally distant relationship. They become adept at managing day-to-day responsibilities without addressing deeper emotional needs. The marriage becomes more about cohabitation and convenience than connection.

This stage is characterized by:

- Routine-driven interactions (raising children, finances, chores)
- Emotional numbness rather than conflict.
- Avoidance of meaningful conversations

3. The Re-Evaluation or Acceptance Stage

In this stage, spouses either choose to re-invest in their marriage or accept the status quo indefinitely. Some may decide to seek personal happiness within the relationship without expecting significant changes from their partner. Others may pursue separation if dissatisfaction becomes unbearable.

This stage is characterized by:

- A turning point for either renewal or permanent acceptance
- Reflection on personal and marital goals
- Openness to new possibilities

This stage is characterized by:

- Routine-driven interactions (raising children, finances, chores)
- Emotional numbness rather than conflict.
- Avoidance of meaningful conversations

The Settling Phase Meta Program

Several years ago in Dundee in Scotland during the school summer holidays, children get taken to the Russian circus that would come to town to entertain.

There will be several perfomances, trapeze artists, clowns, ball jugglers and the rest. Sometimes the children will see dancing bears, see lions, lion tamers or elephants and people sitting in the back of elephants, elephant standing.

And it would fascinate the children how these huge animals could behave so well coordinated and be tamed in such manners.

Truth is, elephants can be tamed.

When a circus decides that it's time to bring a new elephant into its ranks, perhaps an old elephant is getting a little bit older. They'll go to one of the game drives, in Africa somewhere, perhaps Kenya, and they will pick up a young baby elephant who's perhaps lost his parents to poachers.

The circus master will then pay to have their elephants shipped back to their main geographical location, to their circus training ground, and they'll put a chain like a neck chain around the elephant's neck and padlock it and then hammer a really thick pecker into the ground and they'll put a chain around the picker.

The elephant grows, it grows in size and grows in strength, and it learns how to dance and learns how to walk around in circles.

Fast forward 20 years later. This huge, fully grown elephant, though, is walking round and round in circles inside of the circus arena.
But the second that you put a chain around the elephants neck and tighter to peck on the ground. The elephant sits down and goes nowhere because it knows from experience that it's not strong enough to break free from the peg.

The Settling Phase in marriage is a critical period where partners begin to adjust to long-term patterns, for better or worse. It's during this phase that one partner may become "tamed" or conditioned into behaviors that they initially found uncomfortable but later accept as the norm.

In circuses, baby elephants are tied to a strong stake in the ground with a heavy chain. At first, the elephant resists, pulling and struggling to break free.

However, after repeated failed attempts, the elephant eventually accepts that escape is impossible. Even as it grows into a powerful adult capable of breaking free effortlessly, it remains tied to the same small stake, no longer attempting to resist. The elephant has been conditioned into believing that it cannot escape, even when it can.

In the Settling Phase, one partner might find themselves subtly "tamed" into accepting certain behaviors, expectations, or treatment they were initially uncomfortable with. This could be due to:

- Repeated emotional conditioning (e.g., "This is just how relationships are")
- Guilt or fear of conflict (e.g., "I don't want to rock the boat")
- Gradual erosion of personal boundaries
- Normalizing discomfort because it has become familiar

For example, a wife who initially values open communication may find herself in a marriage where her husband withdraws emotionally when there is conflict. At first, she tries to engage him, but over time, she learns that expressing her feelings leads to rejection or silence. Eventually, she stops trying, just like the elephant stops pulling at the stake.

Similarly, a husband who once valued shared decision-making may find himself in a marriage where his opinions are constantly dismissed. Over time, he stops voicing them altogether, believing it's pointless to try—just like the elephant that no longer tests the strength of the chain.

Reasons for Settling

1. Emotional Fatigue and Resignation

After repeated failed attempts to change a situation or be understood, a partner may give up and accept the status quo. This can lead to emotional disconnection and settling into a passive or indifferent relationship dynamic.

2. Emotional and Behavioral Conditioning

Over time, spouses adapt to each other's reactions. If one partner frequently criticizes or withdraws, the other may learn to suppress their true feelings to avoid conflict. Small compromises become habits, and soon, partners accept behaviors they once resisted.

3. Loss of Individual Identity

One or both partners may sacrifice personal passions, friendships, or self-expression for the sake of the marriage. This can lead to feelings of resentment or stagnation, making them feel "stuck" in the marriage.

4. Societal or Cultural Conditioning

Cultural and religious beliefs may pressure individuals to "endure" rather than challenge issues in their marriage. Some partners may believe that it's their duty to accept discomfort rather than demand change.

5. Guilt & Fear of Not Prioritizing the Children

Some spouses feel guilty for leaving their kids to focus on their spouse, believing that children must always come first.

6. The Illusion of Stability Over Growth

Many couples equate lack of conflict with a successful marriage, leading them to avoid necessary growth. They may fear that questioning or disrupting the current dynamic will lead to instability, so they choose to settle instead.

7. Normalization of Unhealthy Patterns

If certain behaviors (e.g., lack of affection, poor communication, avoidance) go unchallenged, they become the new normal. Over time, what was once unacceptable becomes "just the way things are."

8. Spousal Use of PPP to CCC

In some marriages, one spouse leverages their power, position, or privilege to convince, coerce, or control the other, leading to an unhealthy Settling Phase where the affected partner gradually accepts behaviors they once resisted. This can manifest through:

- Emotional power: using emotional manipulation (guilt, silent treatment, gaslighting) to make the other comply.
- Financial Control: The breadwinner may use money as a tool to dictate decisions, making the other feel powerless or dependent.

- Cultural or Religious Justifications: Some partners misuse tradition or faith to demand submission or enforce rigid gender roles, causing the other to settle into an identity that suppresses their true self.
- Decision-Making Domination: When one spouse always overrules or dismisses the other's opinions, the affected partner may stop contributing, settling into passive acceptance.
- Sexual Coercion: A spouse may use guilt, obligation, or intimidation to force intimacy, rather than fostering mutual desire and emotional connection.

Over time, the controlled partner "**settles**" into the belief that resistance is futile, leading to emotional withdrawal and loss of self-confidence.

Settlers Common Phrases

1. 'I just want peace to reign'
2. 'Whatever you want, whatever you say.'
3. 'I'm fine...I'm okay.'
4. 'I have to be submissive.'
5. 'I don't want to be tagged Controlling.'
6. 'What am I supposed to do?'

Five Common Markers of the Settling Phase

1. Physically Present, but Mentally & Emotionally Absent

2. Near but Unreachable

3. Emotionally Unavailable, Unimaginably Feels Entitled

4. Publicly Endearing, Privately Unloving

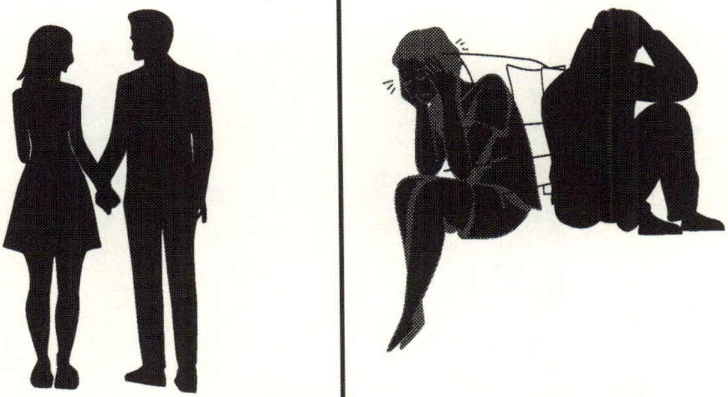

5. Perfects Their State with Roles & Responsibilities

OR

Masks Their State With Raising Children & Activities

Two Types of Settlers

1. Those Who Choose to "Settle" Forever

- These spouses accept their reality as permanent, even though they are unhappy.
- They may stay due to fear, cultural/religious beliefs, financial dependence, or concern for children.
- Over time, they become emotionally numb, resigned, or convince themselves that things are "not that bad."
- They often prioritize stability over personal fulfillment, leading to a stagnant marriage.

2. Those Who "Settle" for a While Until They Can Leave

- These spouses recognize their dissatisfaction but bide their time until they are emotionally, financially, or logistically ready to exit.
- They may strategically plan their departure—saving money, waiting for children to grow, or seeking external support.
- Some remain physically present but emotionally detached, leading to a marriage of convenience rather than connection.
- Once they find the right opportunity, they leave to reclaim their independence and happiness.

The Overlap Between Pushing & Settling

The Pushing Phase is marked by power struggles, disagreements, and adjustments. However, as couples learn to compromise and accept each other's differences, they may gradually enter the Settling Phase, where they begin to establish a rhythm, whether pleasant or unpleasant, in their marriage. Despite this shift, occasional conflicts from the Pushing Phase may resurface, especially during times of stress or change.

A couple may feel like they are making progress, only to face setbacks that temporarily pull them back into old disagreements. Likewise, a spouse who has grown accustomed to the monotony of the marriage may reach a breaking point when their patience is tested beyond its limits, compelling them to re-enter the Pushing Phase in an effort to provoke change.

The overlap here often signals a critical juncture in the marriage, where intervention, such as counseling or structured dialogue is essential to prevent permanent disengagement.

Tools & Recommended Strategies

Unlike the elephant, humans have the ability to become aware of conditioning and break free from it. Couples must recognize unhealthy patterns and have open conversations to realign with what is healthy and fulfilling for both partners.

Just like the circus elephant that *could* break free but doesn't, many spouses remain emotionally stuck in patterns that make them unhappy. However, unlike elephants, humans have the power to change their reality once they recognize it.

Here are practical ways to treat the Settling Phase:

1. Recognize the "Chain"

The first step is to identify the patterns that have been normalized but you feel uncomfortable about. Ask yourself:

- What behaviors have I accepted that go against my core values?
- What do I feel trapped in, and when did I start settling for it?
- Am I staying silent, accommodating, or avoiding conflict to keep peace at the cost of my well-being?

For instance, if you always say "yes" to avoid upsetting your spouse, you will realize that you may lose your voice over time.

2. Loosen the Chain with Honest Conversations

Once you recognize the conditioning going on, it's time to have a conversation. Silence reinforces the pattern—but speaking up is the first step toward change.

How to approach the conversation:

- Choose a calm moment to talk, **not during conflict**.
- Express concerns without blame: Use NFN approach.

"*I've noticed that I have stopped expressing my thoughts because I feel unheard. I don't want this to continue.*"
"I feel....." or "I observe...."

- Be open to feedback and listen to your partner's perspective as well.

3. Test the Strength of the Chain

Conditioning happens when personal boundaries are repeatedly crossed. Re-establishing boundaries is key.

- Identify non-negotiables—things you are no longer willing to compromise.
- Enforce them with consistent actions, not just words.
- Be firm but loving. Boundaries are not ultimatums; they are guidelines for a healthier relationship.

For example, if as a husband you have been conditioned to suppress your emotions because your wife dismisses them, you can say, *"I need to be able to express how I feel without being shut down. This is important to me."*

4. Pull Gently Against the Chain

Change doesn't happen overnight. Breaking free from conditioning starts with small, intentional acts of resistance.

- If you've been avoiding confrontation, practice speaking up about small things first.
- If you've accepted emotional neglect, start seeking connection and affection again.
- If you've given up personal goals or dreams, take small steps to reclaim them.

If as a wife, you stopped making decisions independently, start by choosing a restaurant for date nights instead of always deferring.

5. Rebuild Confidence: The Chain is Weak.

Conditioning creates learned helplessness—the false belief that things cannot change. Breaking free requires rebuilding confidence in personal agency.

- Surround yourself with people who encourage growth.
- Remind yourself of past times you successfully set boundaries or made changes.
- Affirm that discomfort is part of growth—lean into it.

6. Seeking Professional Support to Help Cut the Chain

Sometimes, breaking free from an unhealthy pattern requires outside perspective and guidance. A counselor or coach can help both of you see what you may have become blind to and offer more tools for change.

Conclusion

The chain was never strong!
The chain was never as strong as it seemed. The only thing keeping the elephant tied was the belief that it couldn't break free.
Similarly, in marriage, partners must recognize that they are not powerless - change is possible when they **choose** to take action.

While the Settling Phase can feel like a dead end, it is also an opportunity for reflection and renewal. The good news is that couples who recognize they are in this phase can take intentional steps to revive their relationship and move toward the Growing Phase—where true partnership, joy, and deep connection are restored.

THE GROWING PHASE

Clara & Caleb

The restaurant hummed with a soft jazz melody, its golden lighting casting a warm glow over the elegantly set tables. The air was rich with the aroma of seared steak, garlic butter, and red wine, blending into a perfect ambiance of intimacy. A large window beside their table framed the city skyline, where distant lights flickered like stars.

Caleb reached across the table, his fingers gently intertwining with Clara's. His grip was warm, familiar, and reassuring– Clara smiled, her eyes crinkling at the corners, a beautiful sign of the years they had shared.

"Can you believe it?" Clara mused, swirling her wine glass slightly. "Twenty-eight years, Caleb. It feels like yesterday you walked up to me with that nervous smile at the bookstore."

Caleb chuckled, shaking his head. "Nervous? I was terrified. You were standing there, so effortlessly beautiful, lost in a poetry book. I had to clear my throat three times before you even noticed me."

She laughed softly, squeezing his hand. "And when you finally spoke, you said—"

"'Do you believe in love at first sight, or should I trip over something dramatic so you'll remember me?'" Caleb finished, grinning.

Clara threw her head back, her laughter light and genuine. "It was so cheesy, yet so perfect."

He gazed at her, the candlelight reflecting in her deep brown eyes. "And yet, here we are..." he stuttered and fought back a tear. "After kids, careers, and many fights... here we are." His voice lowered into a soft murmur. "I never imagined a day like this would come again."

Clara lifted his hand to her lips, kissing his knuckles gently. "Neither did I." Her voice wavered slightly, emotion thickening her words. "But tonight is not for tears and regrets, it's for growth and new memories."

"Yes, it's for growth." he smiled heartily.

"You still look at me the way you did back then, Caleb. Like I'm the only woman in the world."

"You are the only woman in my world," he said firmly.

“Even when time paints silver in our hair and carves wisdom into our skin, my love for you won’t change. It will only deepen, Clara.”

Her eyes glistened as she whispered, “You always know what to say.”

Caleb smirked. “Well, I’ve not said much in the last few years, I’m seizing every moment I get, going forward.” He leaned forward, brushing his fingers across her cheek before tucking a loose strand of hair behind her ear. “Do you remember the song we danced to the last time we came here.”

“How can I forget? It was twenty-five years ago, our second wedding anniversary did!” Clara giggled, shaking her head.

Caleb chuckled, his eyes twinkling with nostalgia. "I requested that song again tonight. Just for us."

Clara’s gaze softened as she looked at him. "You didn’t."

"I did." He leaned back, lifting his wine glass with a playful glint in his eyes. "I figured we deserve a little reminder of what started it all."

Before Clara could respond, the soft strumming of a familiar melody filled the air. Her breath hitched. It was their song—the one they had swayed to all those years ago, wrapped in each other's arms, lost in their own world.

She turned to look at Caleb, warmth spreading through her chest. "You still remember."

"Every word. Every note. Every moment." He stood, extending his hand toward her. "May I have this dance, Mrs. Anderson?"

Clara laughed, shaking her head but placing her hand in his anyway. "I can't believe you planned this."

"I had to." He pulled her gently to her feet and led her to the small dance floor near their table. The restaurant wasn't crowded, but a few diners smiled in admiration as they watched the couple.

As the music enveloped them, Caleb wrapped an arm around Clara's waist, drawing her close. "You know, you still fit perfectly in my arms."

She smiled, resting her head against his chest. "I never stopped loving the way you hold me."

They swayed in unison, their movements slow and effortless, as if time had rewound to that night twenty-five years ago. Caleb hummed along to the tune, his voice low but steady. Clara closed her eyes, relishing the moment.

After a while, she pulled back slightly, her eyes searching his. "Caleb, is this change real? I don't want to go back to what we were."

He exhaled, brushing his thumb over her knuckles. "It's real. And because of the help and counseling we are getting, I am more confident things will be different now. I want to make every moment count with you."

Clara studied him for a moment, searching for any hesitation in his eyes. But all she found was sincerity, a quiet determination she hadn't seen in years. "I am doing same. No more taking you for granted. No more ignoring your needs. You will never feel unseen again. I commit to doing better from now on."

His heart swelled, emotion tightening his throat. "Clara..."

"Yes, Caleb." She looked at him in admiration.

"That means more to me than you know."

She nodded, a tear slipping down her cheek, but this time, it wasn't sadness—it was hope. "Just dance with me."

"We will keep building, one step at a time. We will keep prioritizing each other."

"It only gets better from here."

They danced, wrapped in the melody, wrapped in each other. No past hurts, no missed moments—only the promise of a love renewed, stronger than ever.

The song faded, and they slowly made their way back to their table, hands intertwined. Their meal was already served, steam rising from the perfectly plated dishes. Caleb pulled out her chair before taking his seat.

As she took a bite, Clara sighed contentedly. "Mmm, just the way I like it."

As they ate, their conversation flowed effortlessly, laughter blending with reminiscence. The weight that had once burdened their hearts felt lighter now, as if love had carved out space for something new—a fresh start, a renewed promise.

By the time dessert arrived, Clara reached for his hand again. "Before our next counseling session tomorrow..." She paused and waited for him to look at her.

"Yes... what is it?"

"There's something I want to show you when we get home tonight." She winked.

"Mrs. Anderson, the mischief in your eyes is suspicious. What are you planning?"

She leaned back on her chair, angled to the left and gave him a dark stare. "You will just have to wait."

THE GROWING PHASE

Est. 0yr - forever

The Growing Phase is a phase where both partners choose a lifetime of continuous learning, growing, and increasing in knowledge about how to treat each other better, grow their union and live flourishing lives. They have a positive disposition towards new insights, especially when such makes them better partners.

Partners in the Growing Phase have overtime, from the Learning Phase built a pattern where they are constantly reviewing their opinions, investigating their choices, checking to see if they are empowering their union or sabotaging it, and resolving to only take decisions that are geared towards their common good.

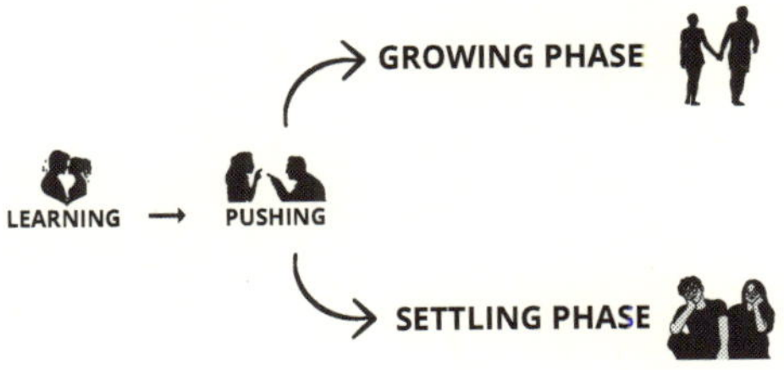

Peculiar Traits

The partners

- are open to learning and improvement. They actively seek new insights to strengthen their relationship.
- are intentional about growth. They don't wait for problems to arise before working on their marriage.
- give each other the freedom to express thoughts, feelings, and concerns openly and constructively.
- take time to address issues calmly and work towards solutions rather than blame.
- prioritize deep emotional connection and vulnerability.
- maintain habits like date nights, check-ins, and shared activities. They see such as marriage fitness routines.
- support each other's personal goals while nurturing the marriage.
- embrace change and navigate life's transitions together holding each other's hands every step of the way.
- uplift each other, celebrate successes, and offer comfort during challenges.

Three Stages in the Growing Phase

1. *The Awakening Stage*

This is the stage where the partners recognize the need for growth. It usually happens in the transition from Learning Phase to Pushing Phase.

They become aware of tendencies in them that may not favorably serve the marriage. They recognize their imprints or meta-programs that may sabotage their desired future and as a result, they subject themselves to intentional learning and effort to dropping habits that are not helpful and picking new profitable ones.

This stage is characterized by:

- A shift from reactive love (responding to issues as they come) to proactive love (learning and growing before problems arise).
- Willingness to reflect on past mistakes and acknowledge areas that need improvement.
- Curiosity and openness to new insights about marriage, personal development, and relational dynamics.

2. *The Action Stage*

This stage involves implementing growth strategies. It's the understanding that awareness alone is not enough, so the couples put knowledge into practice by changing behaviors, deepening communication, and strengthening their bond. When there is conflict, they usually apply the Pause & Process rule by take a short break, reflect, and return to the conversation with a solution-focused mindset.

This stage is characterized by:

- Learning how to listen actively, resolve conflicts healthily, and express love in meaningful ways.
- Creating consistent routines for connection, such as regular date nights, shared learning experiences, or joint goal-setting.
- Responding to each other with patience, empathy, and understanding rather than reacting impulsively.
- Checking in with each other about progress and being open to constructive feedback.

3. *The Flourishing Stage*

This stage is where growth becomes a way of life, and the relationship experiences deep fulfillment, renewed passion, and mutual empowerment. The couple no longer sees growth as an obligation but as a shared commitment to an enriched marriage.

This stage is characterized by:

- A strong sense of "we" - Both partners feel like a united team, balancing individual identities with a shared purpose.
- Increased intimacy, both emotionally and physically, as they continue investing in each other.
- They think beyond the present, aiming to create a lasting impact for their family, children, and future generations.
- They begin to inspire, guide, and encourage other couples in their circle.

The Growing Phase is not about achieving perfection but about embracing a lifelong commitment to learning, evolving, and deepening love. Every couple moves through these three stages at their own

pace but, those who intentionally invest in their marriage will experience a rich, fulfilling, and enduring union.

The Overlap Between Settling & Growing

In the Settling Phase, the pushing spouse, having grown weary of unmet expectations and emotional exertion, stops advocating for change and instead adjusts to the reality of the marriage as it is, rather than as they hoped it would be. This is not necessarily a conscious decision but rather a survival response, protecting oneself from further disappointment.

However, a couple can experience both Settling and Growing Phases simultaneously, particularly when one spouse has resolved to accept things as they are, while the other remains committed to continuous growth.

In some cases, the growth-oriented partner's positive influence can reignite the other spouse's willingness to learn and grow, pulling them out of Settling. But, if the Settling partner resists change, the Growing partner may experience frustration, leading them to either adjust expectations, continue growing independently, or reconsider the viability of the relationship.

The Overlap Between Learning & Growing

A couple that has moved from Learning to Growing experiences a seamless and enriching overlap. They actively apply lessons learned and maintain a mindset of continuous improvement.

This overlap creates a healthy relationship ecosystem where both partners are invested in their collective well-being, increasing intimacy, trust, and shared goals. Couples in this dynamic often serve as role models for others, exemplifying what a flourishing marriage can look like.

Marital phases are not linear; they are fluid and often intersect. Understanding these overlaps can help couples navigate challenges, reinforce their commitment, and create an environment where both partners feel supported. The ultimate goal is to transition into the Growing Phase, where continuous learning and mutual investment become the foundation of a thriving relationship.

Seven Tools & Strategies Growers Deploy

1. Effective Communication Tools

- Active Listening - Giving full attention, making eye contact, and validating each other's feelings.
- "I" Statements - Expressing concerns without blaming (e.g., "I feel unheard when..." instead of "You never listen").
- Check-in Conversations - Regular discussions about emotions, expectations, and relationship progress.

2. Conflict Resolution Strategies

- Pause & Process Method - Taking a break before reacting in heated situations.
- Fair Fighting Rules - Avoiding name-calling, interrupting, or bringing up past mistakes.
- Compromise & Negotiation - Finding win-win solutions rather than insisting on being right.

3. Emotional & Physical Intimacy Builders

- Daily Affection Rituals - Small gestures like hugs, kisses, and kind words to reinforce connection.
- Love Language Alignment - Understanding and practicing each other's preferred ways of receiving love.
- Deep Conversations - Going beyond surface-level talks to discuss dreams, fears, and long-term goals.

4. Growth-Oriented Habits

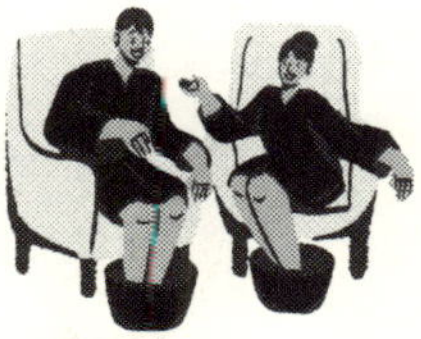

- Regular Date Nights - Keeping romance alive with intentional one-on-one time.
- Shared Learning Experiences - Attending workshops, marriage seminars, couples' retreats, reading books, or listening to relationship podcasts together.
- Couples' Vision Board - Setting and visualizing long-term goals for their marriage and family.

5. Individual & Mutual Self Development

- Personal Growth Commitment - Supporting each other's ambitions, hobbies, and career goals.

- Marriage Accountability Partners - Having a Marital coach or mentor for guidance and encouragement.
- Journaling & Reflection - Writing

thoughts, challenges, and gratitude moments to track growth.

6. Spiritual & Value-Based Anchors

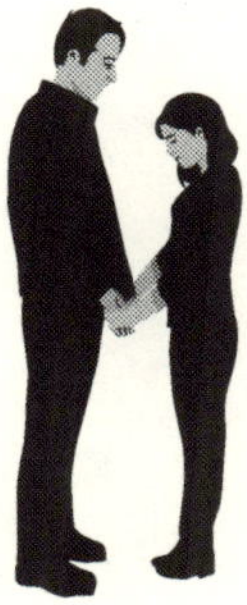

- Praying Together - Strengthening the relationship through shared spiritual practices.
- Ethical Decision-Making - Basing marriage choices on shared values and principles.
- Community & Service - Giving back together to strengthen their bond and impact others positively.

7. Self-Care & Individual Well-being

- They recognize that a healthy marriage starts with two healthy individuals.

- By prioritizing personal well-being—physically, emotionally, and spiritually—they bring their best selves into the relationship, reducing stress and fostering a balanced, thriving partnership.

The Significance of a Marital Coach

Marriage is a lifelong journey that evolves through different seasons. While love and commitment are essential, they are not always enough to navigate the complexities of a partnership successfully. This is where a marital coach plays a crucial role. A marital coach is a trained professional who provides guidance, support, and practical tools to help couples strengthen their relationship, overcome challenges, and build a thriving marriage.

Below are six reasons why having a marital coach matter.

- Objective Guidance: Unlike family or friends who may be emotionally involved, a marital coach offers an unbiased perspective. They help couples see issues clearly and provide solutions that align with their unique relationship dynamics.
- Improved Communication: Many marital conflicts stem from miscommunication. A coach teaches couples how to listen actively, express themselves effectively, and resolve conflicts in healthy ways.
- Conflict Resolution Skills: Disagreements are inevitable, but unresolved conflicts can weaken a marriage. A marital coach equips couples with strategies to handle disagreements constructively, preventing resentment from taking root.
- Personal and Relational Growth: A strong marriage is built on the growth of both individuals. Marital coaching helps partners recognize personal areas of improvement, fostering self-awareness and emotional intelligence.

- Accountability and Support: A coach holds couples accountable for the changes they want to implement in their marriage. This accountability keeps them committed to progress, even when challenges arise.
- Preventative Care: Many couples wait until their marriage is in crisis before seeking help. However, marital coaching is beneficial for maintaining a healthy relationship, preventing minor issues from escalating into major problems.

'Growers' & Marital Coaching

The Growing Phase in marriage is where couples intentionally invest in their relationship. They are aware of the growth they witnessed as a result of the investments they made in their career, in their children, in their businesses and social connections. These experiences have taught them that nothing just happens, whatever you give attention to, thrives and whatever you don't give attention to dies. They recognize that marriage is not just about coexisting but about continuously nurturing their bond. The bond and connection they desire won't just happen by wishing for it, so they see the guidance of a professional marital coach as a powerful strategy that for marital bliss and mutual flourishing. By engaging with a marital coach, couples

- Deepen their connection by learning how to understand and meet each other's needs.
- Stay adaptable as life transitions, such as career changes, parenting, or aging, bring new challenges.
- Develop resilience so they can navigate difficult seasons without losing sight of their love and commitment.

In essence, having a marital coach is not a sign of weakness but a sign of wisdom and commitment. It is one of the best investments couples can make in their relationship, ensuring they continue to flourish together, regardless of life's ups and downs.

Conclusion

Embracing Your Marriage Journey with Intentionality

Marriage is a journey, not a destination. As you reflect on The Four Phases of Marriage: the Learning Phase, Pushing Phase, Settling Phase, and Growing Phase, remember that each stage comes with its own set of challenges, lessons, and opportunities for growth. No matter which phase you find yourself in, the key to a thriving marriage lies in intentionality, commitment, and continuous effort.

Understanding these phases equips you with the wisdom to navigate difficulties, the patience to embrace growth, and the joy of deepening your connection with your spouse. Marriage is not about avoiding struggles; it's about facing them together, learning from them, and emerging stronger as a couple.

What's Next?

- Identify Your Current Phase: Take a moment to assess where you and your spouse are in your marriage journey. Recognizing your current phase allows you to be more intentional about what your relationship needs.

- Implement the Right Strategies: Each phase requires different approaches. If you're in the Learning Phase, focus on building a strong foundation. In the Pushing Phase, commit to working through challenges as a team. In the Settling Phase, guard against complacency and reignite passion. And if you're in the Growing Phase, keep nurturing and investing in your relationship.

- Communicate and Reconnect: Have open conversations with your spouse about your journey together. A thriving marriage is built on consistent, honest, and loving communication.

- Seek Support and Growth: Growth doesn't happen in isolation. Consider seeking guidance from mentors, marital coaches, or counseling programs to strengthen your bond and gain fresh insights.

- Keep God at the Center: A marriage rooted in faith, love, and grace stands the test of time. Seek wisdom, pray together, and trust that your journey is unfolding with divine purpose.

Your Marriage Can Flourish!

No matter where you are in your marriage, you have the power to flourish, deepen your love, and build a relationship that lasts a lifetime. Each phase is an opportunity to learn, strengthen, and grow together. With intentionality, commitment, and the right mindset, your marriage can become a beacon of love, joy, and partnership, a story worth celebrating.

The journey continues. Step forward with purpose, embrace the season you are in, and choose to grow together, every single day.

Discover Your Marital Phase and Stage

Understanding these phases—Learning, Pushing, Settling, and Growing—is the first step to building a fulfilling and resilient marriage. However, knowledge alone is not enough; personal application is key.

Every marriage is unique, and couples may find themselves at different phases based on their personal experiences, level of effort, and external influences. Even within a phase, the depth of the experience may vary, meaning that two couples in the Pushing Phase may not necessarily be dealing with the same intensity of challenges. This is why taking a marital assessment is essential, it will help you pinpoint exactly where you are and what strategies will work best for you.

Why Take the Marital Phase Assessment?

1. Clarity: It provides an objective understanding of where your marriage currently stands.
2. Direction: It helps you identify whether you need to focus on building skills, addressing conflicts, reconnecting, or maintaining growth.
3. Customized Treatment Plan: Based on your results, you'll receive recommendations tailored to your specific phase and stage within that phase.
4. Hope and Encouragement: No matter what phase you are in, there are always steps to take toward a healthier and stronger marriage.

How the Assessment Works

The assessment consists of a series of thought-provoking questions designed to evaluate:

- Your current level of satisfaction in marriage
- The frequency and intensity of conflicts
- Your communication patterns
- Emotional and physical connection
- Your level of personal and mutual growth

Once you complete the assessment, you'll be able to identify your current phase and determine your specific stage within that phase.

After identifying your phase, refer back to the corresponding section in this book and apply the recommended treatment strategies. If you find that deeper intervention is needed, consider seeking counseling or coaching to guide you through the transformation process.

Remember, your marriage is a journey, not a destination. Knowing where you are today gives you the power to take intentional steps toward the marriage you desire. Take the assessment, embrace the process, and commit to growing together!

Click the link below for the assessment.
https://juwonodutayo.com/marital-phase-assessment/

Epilogue

"It's good to see both of you here again. You look different. Tell me, how has it been? You both look lighter and happier."

Clara reached for Caleb's hand, intertwining their fingers. "Honestly, it's been transformative."

"There is a major shift." Caleb nodded in agreement. "We had thought there was no hope for us because of how long we had been stuck in a cycle of frustration and resentment. But since we embraced the tools and strategies we discussed, I feel like we just got married."

"Our home feels different. Our sons were home last weekend. They didn't want to leave because of how much fun we were all having."

The coach leaned in, intrigued. "That's wonderful to hear! What specific changes have you noticed?"

Clara smiled. "For one, we've become more mindful of our communication. I used to get defensive at the slightest critique, but now, I remind myself that Caleb is my partner, not my opponent."

Caleb chuckled. "And that's made a huge difference. We've built a habit of checking in with each other daily, simple things like 'How was your day?' and 'Is there anything on your mind?' These small conversations have deepened our bond."

"Amazing."

“I used to avoid difficult conversations.” Clara giggled.

Caleb squeezed her hand. "I think what helped the most was recognizing that we're on the same team. It's not me versus Clara—it's us against the issue. That shift in mindset has been life changing."

The coach smiled. “Have you noticed any changes in how you connect emotionally and physically?"

Clara's eyes twinkled. "Oh, absolutely. Do you want all the juicy details, or should I keep it PG13 for you?”

The coach laughed. “Let's keep it PG13.”

“Okay then, let's just say the fireworks that happen after the date nights makes me feel like sixteen again.”

“Very interesting.”

Caleb added, "For me, the biggest change is feeling seen and valued. Before, we coexisted, but now, we truly experience each other.”

The coach beamed. "That's the essence of the Growing Phase—intentionality, commitment, and rediscovering the joy in your marriage. I'm incredibly proud of the progress you've made.

Clara's voice was soft but filled with conviction. "We're deeply grateful. We're not just surviving marriage anymore; we're thriving in it, and we are flourishing together."

Credit: Graphics from Canva Free Images

Made in the USA
Columbia, SC
28 March 2025

55809951R10076